Idealistic for utopia   there are other possibilities ☑
Book is pessimistic
  Humor- Subtle resistance, quiet
        Coping mechanism

Why octopus?   grow limbs
    Smart, high IQ

② Very specific
   More details- More visceral, realistic
   Absurd + fantastical world   ⟶ shocking contrast
      Problems are jarringly realistic, things close to us

ALSO BY BRENDA SHAUGHNESSY

So Much Synth

Our Andromeda

Human Dark with Sugar

Interior with Sudden Joy

THE OCTOPUS MUSEUM

THE OCTOPUS MUSEUM

Poems

BRENDA SHAUGHNESSY

ALFRED A. KNOPF, NEW YORK, 2019

THIS IS A BORZOI BOOK
PUBLISHED BY ALFRED A. KNOPF

Published in the United States by Alfred A. Knopf,
a division of Penguin Random House LLC, New York,
and in Canada by Random House of Canada, a division
of Penguin Random House Canada Limited, Toronto.

www.aaknopf.com

Knopf, Borzoi Books, and the colophon are
registered trademarks of Penguin Random House LLC.

Library of Congress Cataloging-in-Publication Data
Names: Shaughnessy, Brenda, 1970– author.
Title: The octopus museum : poems / Brenda Shaughnessy.
Description: New York : Knopf, 2019.
Identifiers: LCCN 2018036768 (print) | LCCN 2018038674 (ebook) |
ISBN 9780525655657 (hardcover) | ISBN 9780525655664 (ebook)
Subjects: | BISAC: POETRY / American / General.
Classification: LCC PS3569.H353 (ebook) | LCC PS3569.H353 A6 2019 (print) |
DDC 811/.54—DC23
LC record available at https://lccn.loc.gov/2018036768

Jacket photograph by Kim Keever

Jacket design by Carol Devine Carson

Manufactured in Canada

Published March 19, 2019
Second Printing, October 2019

For Simone

If a society permits one portion of its citizenry to be menaced

or destroyed, then, very soon, no one in that society is safe.

The forces thus released in the people can never be held in check,

but run their devouring course, destroying the very foundations

which it was imagined they would save.

—JAMES BALDWIN

When you lie dead, no one will remember you

For you have no share in the Muses' roses.

Quotes chosen?

—SAPPHO, Fragment 33

☆

VISITOR'S GUIDE
TO THE OM EXHIBITS

The OM has five exhibition spaces, with another three currently under construction.

"TO SERVE MAN":
RITUALS OF THE LATE ANTHROPOCENE COLONY

FOUND OBJECTS/LOST SUBJECTS:
A RETROSPECTIVE

PERMANENT COLLECTION:
ARCHIVE OF PRE-EXISTING CONDITIONS

THE OCTOPUS MUSEUM

Identity & Community (There Is No "I" in "Sea")

I don't want to be surrounded by people. Or even one person. But I don't want to
   always be alone.
The answer is to become my own pet, hungry for plenty in a plentiful place.
There is no true solitude, only only.
At seaside, I have that familiar sense of being left out, too far to glean the secret: *how*
   go in?
What an inhuman surface the sea has, always open.
I'm too afraid to go in. I give no yes.
Full of shame, but refuse to litter ever. I pick myself up.
Wind has power. Sun has power. What is power's source?

There's no privacy outside. We've invaded it.   *Alliteration*
There is no life outside empire. All paradise is performance for people
   who pay.
Perhaps I'm an invader and feel I haven't paid.
What a waste, to have lost everything in mind.

                                          jealous

Watching three mom-like women try to go in, I'm green— I want to join them.
But they are not my women. I join them, apologizing.
They splash away from me—they're their pod. People are alien.
I'm an unknown story, erasing myself with seawater.
There goes my honey and fog, my shoulders and legs.

WHAT What could be queerer than this queer tug-lust for what already is, who already am,
   but other of it?   *fragmented grammar*
Happens? That kind of desire anymore?
Oh I am that queer thing pulling and greener than the blue sea. I'm new with envy.
Beauty washing over itself. No reflection. No claim. Nothing to see.
If there's anything bluer than the ocean it's its greenness. It's its turquoise blood,
   mixing me.

I was a woman alone in the sea.
Don't tell anybody, I tell myself.
Don't try to remember this. Don't document it.
Remember: write down to not-document it.   *Key*

| 3

GALLERY OF

A DREAMING SPECIES

No Traveler Returns

[handwritten: human body]

I was like you once, a sealed plastic bag of water filters floating on the sea.

I thought my numbers proved my time and space on earth.

I thought having children was a way of creating more love.

[handwritten: ☆]

I thought thoughts I was ashamed to speak in case they were what everyone already thought or in case they were unthinkable thoughts nobody would dare think much less say which would blow up the world everyone else had to live in if I said them.

[handwritten: ↓]

[handwritten: Becomes more extreme]

I muddled that distinction to extinction—pure silence not a piece of peace and a breathlessness not of wonder but blackthroat, choking on backwash.

Once a wild tentacled screaming creature every inch a kissed lip of a beloved place, a true and relentless mind, all heart if heart is a dumb hope of reusable pump.

What was it you said that made me think I was like you once?

Remember the last terrifying moments? You clenched up and wanted me to be completely open.

We'd broken up (remember such terms? Such luxury? We thought breaking up a kind of preservation.) and to cut off circulation decided to sever at the place where our hair had grown together.

An axe, a pair of kitchen scissors. That rusty axe fully fatigued and scissors which cut raw chicken bacteria into everything it touched.

[handwritten: innuendo]

Nothing did the trick. To come apart we'd have to come, together; and so I tried to make you come; you said it was our last time so you'd remember it.

You cried out, then cried and I cried and I hardened against you, then softened, then wished we could go back, wanted to love you like before, twisted myself like nobody's pile of wires.

Did you try to make me come, and I couldn't, wouldn't? Or did I give you that and let you let me go?

———————

And there will be no other way to be, once this way's gone. The last song on earth, the last jellybean. Last because nobody wanted it, or everybody sang it, till the end.

Once this day in November's over never another. Each day nothing like the last except that it's the last and that's new, too.

Each moment broken glasses, a covered mirror, foxed. The waste stays in place. The rest disappears. The unrest, too.

There's no way to follow my own mind. My own mind is not leading. I'm unleaded. I'm gasoline.

I'm everything in between this flame and that attracted wind. I forgot my glasses— how will we drink?

Seeing isn't believing if I believe I see better with something I can so easily forget.

And what if I can't forget? I forgot the heft and squirm of my own baby in my arms, in my own womb.

I'll forget anything and call it an accident, match to fuel and breathing it all in as if I'm living normally from day to re-registered day.

Why is it, if I can only remember what I myself experienced, that I can also forget what I experienced? Who records the records and collects the recollections?

I had that baby in my womb for thirty-nine weeks, for three quarters of a year, a full calendar minus summer. An unforgettable summer, each day fucking endless.

Oh I know all the numbers; everything adds up. I've never seen my womb but my doctor has. I never saw that doctor again.

Gift Planet

My six-year-old said, "I don't know time." She already knows it's unknowable. Let it be always a stranger she walks wide around.

I fantasize about outer space as if I have some relation to it besides being an animal in its zoo. No visitors. No matter how far I travel on earth I wind up sitting in rooms.

Wind up running all over towns and streets the same. Then get hungry as anywhere, again. Going anyplace, I think: I never want to go home and I can't wait to be home.

All traveling's a way to imagine having a home to leave or return to.

The shame of never leaving home. The anguish of no home. Changing housekeys on the unchanged ring. The ring is the home, the thing inside trees.

Claiming a tree "mine."

Car feels like a pod, an exoskeleton, a place inside me. Car short for "carapace." ?

I blame the weather, blame myself if the weather is "nice." Tell myself the weather ruined my plans, though it's me ruined the weather's. Climate change?

Plan: like plane like plain like pain/pane. Like planet. Plan acting like an overlay on everything most elemental. Trying to make everything go according to it— feelings, food, flight, ordinariness, the very earth.

Stop already. Stop as if you can. As if you can breathe back in your own baby, your two, your three. Breathe out all the ones you never had. Breathe in one two three. Breathe out all the others.

I don't want to be cremated. I want to be part of earth. Space may be my original home but I only remember here.

I cling to this life. I've taped myself to it like a card on a gift. Happy birthday! Many happy returns and hope it's lots of fun! We miss you! Love, Me.

A gift is always an exchange of energy. Like water boiling, like photosynthesis. Inside the box is a water pitcher and a picture of us together as we were when the photo was taken.   *redundant*

Now it's given. It's only a copy, but the original was a moment and was burned up, caloric.

Simone says before bed, "I'm imagining a strawberry automatically drawn. I dream so much when I'm awake."

 When I learned to tell time I told it. I told it so; I stopped listening to what it tried to tell me: You're already losing everything as you go and go and go.

tell time
  wordplay

Wellness Rituals

You never understood me until you watched me wash the inside of the well, with clean wellwater and invisible soap which dissolves the dirt and then clumps up and floats to the surface, suddenly iridescent.

I net up the greening lumps, skimming. I leave the net out to dry. Within hours the lumps are coagulated and bacterial, dirty heads striated with living question marks, leech-pieces, worm eyes, segments of fertile sediment.

Enough bio-material to assemble themselves into flying animals, little glowing spitballs. They waver off into their new lives. I made them surely as I made my daughter: without knowing how.

uncomprehendable nature

we accept systems but dont know how they work

I washed down the sides with seasponge, as far as my arms could go then lowered myself in the bucket. Down there I used my feet. Scrubbed the stones and cracks of moss and slime and what else? Dead water. New algae. Legs of things.

I held my breath against the earth perfume in case it was infected, and spread my legs to straddle the diameter, my toes clenched on wet grit. My own holes amphibian as ever. Where does my water come from? From myself you know.

I am a self-cleaning animal and my children were born glistening under all the soft trees leaving, breathing. You understand me now; the well was always clean. I clean it anyhow. It is no cleaner now than it was but I am.

Wellness, health   Personal

Future looking back

There Was No Before (Take Arms Against a Sea of Troubles)

✰ Before health insurance there was health, a pre-existing condition before the weird paper-cut-on-the-neck had you eventually getting around in a wheelbarrow pulled by a gentle mule named Sinister. Sure it's metaphoric. Also true.

When I say you, I mean me. Who else can I talk to? Before you were born, the world got along hopelessly without you, lonely without knowing why. The sharp edges of birdsong scraped across the sky gay with fever, no way to bring it down.

On the ground, houses were called homes and homes were called living spaces and they dotted the sick countryside—those near-dead spaces. Dead spaces were called cemeteries back then, too. Dead air was what the interred watched on TV.

Everything was a show, which must go on and on, continuing in sleep rehearsal space. In the morning our dreams were still a mess, nobody knew the blocking, gels melted onto the hot lights, and we could hardly sit through the thing.

media
TV
drama
entertainment

In waking life we said our lines or broke character or looked directly at the lens, and were entertained. We binge-watched ourselves till we believed daybreak was a rerun and the stars a quiet new kind of crime drama that had inaudible singing in it.

———

My child would complain when I didn't let her stay the second half of the pre-school day. "I want to be part of the Lunch Bunch!" though I'd make her her favorite at home. Of course the school had to make it sound fun for kids to be left all day.

I couldn't afford all-day pre-school. Soon nobody could afford it. Before and after-Before, too. Children have always had to stuff their whole selves into the corners pinning their grown-ups. I thought I'd miss her too much anyway, and indeed I do.

short
childish
language

I know nothing about her job these days. Surely she's got a lunch bunch at the staff caf with her break mates. A corner of her own with friends before her second shift. She has so little time outside of work. ✰ *Find a little bit of freedom w/in the prose paragraphs*

Before Sinister came into the family you rolled yourself down, saying *It's all downhill from here*. Which was the same as saying *It's all uphill*. You'd pick up friends, neighbors, exes, along the way and give them rides. You all went downhill fast.

Black children were killed in broad daylight, in parks and streets and in houses and churches and cars. Especially in cars. The law said it wasn't allowed, but it was expressly allowed, encouraged, and unpunished. The law said this was the law, each time a person chose to do it. These were not accidents.

police brutality

This was Before, and we're almost certain it is the same now as Before, only now we don't know the laws. They keep it overtly secret now, as they think we'll think there was no Before. It's not just black children anymore, it's everyone.

———

We didn't all used to have shells. Our skin was soft and easily cut, even a sheet of paper could sever your nerves, become infected, and leave you wheelbarrow-bound. It didn't even matter what was written on the paper.

We could afford our naked flesh, survival-wise, less so if the outer layer of your flesh was dark or part-dark. And there were commonly awful injuries to the softest flesh especially of women and kids where men turned their flesh to weapons.

domestic violence

These were not accidents. These injuries altered the bodies and minds of the women and kids and changed the flesh and spirit of the as-yet-uninjured, too. The threat of flesh harming flesh went beyond flesh.

Because it was the mind of a person that put the harm in motion. A person chose to do it. Women hid in basements, trying to imagine the mind of a man bent on harm. Kids thought they had to do whatever grown-ups told them.

They thought that a man who had a puppy was always nice. Women swaggered in groups downtown and were picked off one by one. Women thought they were the only one every time it happened. Kids stopped remembering whole years.

———

Long before people existed, mollusks were soft plasmic shapes for whom, if you mentioned shells they'd say *Whatever you're talking about is completely alien to me and I am not interested* as if you were trying to sell them, simple Ediacaran bilaterals, a bridge.

After millions of years of disinterested, shell-less floating and sea-floor-attaching, they only developed shells in response to a new scene in the oceans. Predators became invented and the undersea nobodies strategized with zero brains.

evolution

The "new" predators were the first on earth, the first dog to eat dog in this world. Mollusks grew shells, homes, and stayed inside for millions more years, sometimes daring to stick a foot out, footing around for food.

You see these shells on the beach. Or you did before, when we walked on the beach free as birds plucking innards. They are decorative, sheeny little half-compacts— each a grim acquiescence to a new regime, and the first resistance.

When my grandma was little she heard the maxim "It's a dog-eat-dog world" as "It's a doggy dog world." Oh little grandma! Before mollusks were forced to grow shells it *was* doggy-dog out there. But ever since then we're hungry all the time.

We also dream of multiple-ingredient meals. Carrots for dinner two nights a week is not what we imagined when we thought we chose Vegan Paradise, or before when we believed in the feelings of animals but still ate them with relish, hot sauce, mustard, and regret. LoL

We envisioned rainbow salads with cream-free goddess dressing, long, funky grains of every stripe mixed with soups of the world, not a medium-large can of beets per family as a treat on Tuesdays. Fridays we get beans *and* whatever lettuce is lying around. Bitter stems, semi-liquid.

Before, we could always count on at least a heel or two of gluten loaf, but it depends on which cruelty-full Before you're thinking of. Me, I'm thinking of all the Befores, like all old people who have no future.

———

Before our COO learned how to communicate electronically, we thought they were merely naïvely excited about "life on land" (LOL) so we equally naively helped them build COOPS (Cephalo-Octopodal Oceanostomy Pods).

Soon we realized we'd been doubly naive and they'd been zero naive because they used their new land mobility to access the world's Electronic Communication Operating Systems (ECOS) and boy could they type fast.

It became clear that they, the COO (Cephalopod Octopoid Overlords) were taking over. While we were still marveling at the cuteness of YouTube videos showing early COO antics and enjoying the adorableness of their eight-legged smartypants brand,

they had reconfigured the ECOS language, and took over every computer, grid, and control center. We still do not know their language. We think they think we are too stupid to learn it and we know they know they are probably right.

COO read, or rather ingested, the entire internet in a matter of weeks. Who knew their decentralized nervous system, advanced visual acuity, and eight highly sensitive mega-arms would make such quick work in the realm of keystrokes and swipe commands?

It's almost as if we invented this technology to play to their specific evolutionary strengths. They have complex, light-sensitive, four-dimensional, laser vision and we have 20/20 hindsight.

Politically Correct Joke?

The COO renamed itself the CEO (Cephalopod Electro-Overlords)—dropping the *Octopus* nickname as an outdated, human-centric, offensive term that excluded squid, nautiluses, and other potential commanding officers and executives-in-training.

police?

Likewise, COOPS are now called COPS, installed in watchtowers and moats in every human settlement. Most of us work in their salinizing centers. Before, we dumped our waste and garbage into their oceans, and ruined that delicate world.

———

ocean destroyed

Their vast home of millions of years destroyed, the COO came ashore. We knew they were intelligent. They could open jars and pretend to be more poisonous creatures than they, ostensibly, were. We found them darling, delicious.

They don't understand our racism. They change color and blend in. To them, change is only ever considered a natural gift, a condition of being. The real skill is survival. Knowing how to change—not color or mind or body or action but perspective—and refusing to do it is how species vanish. Humans

My shell has become relatively substantial—proportionate to the amount of danger I'm in. I'm a woman. A mother. I am very soft and have so much to protect. Many women and mothers, even the old and weak, have the strongest shells.

Except certain pale women who were extremely wealthy Before. They seem to lack a certain enzyme. Their shells are transparent, bendable, a vinyl-like film, but porous like all they can grow and carry on their backs is a flimsy safety net.

Mine's a cross between hardwood and Corian, the plastic-stone stuff they used to make slightly cheaper kitchen counters. Of course it's not really made of those materials. It's made of me. Thick-middled, silver-streaked, motherfucking furious me.

I don't know about men's shells. They won't tell me and I don't care enough to care. Maybe I blame them for all the years of cluelessness and rampage. Or I'm ashamed of us all and prefer to think mostly about my daughter, how she's getting by.

SPECIAL COLLECTION:

"AS THEY WERE"

The Home Team

I liked Jane's team. I'd bet money on them but it wasn't that kind of thing. Too disorganized, plus it was just lunchtime pickup winterball with deflated goal bulbs and not enough of the good knee-gel to go around. The kids were tough. The kids goofed. Jane shone.

She worried that winterball like a craft, then, like it was nothing, she'd plffft it dead center while everyone else looked sleepy, sidewise, a full surprise every time. Her main move always a low private conversation with the air. Then lightning knees you could never see.

The rest of the team shot sparks on occasion. Tella's swift half-bank could rattle the shoulder of the thickest bulb-guard, and The Brain (a sticky girl in Advanced Graphmatics) had all the angles. We stood in the stands like snipers, trying to see what The Brain saw but never did till the fluke-score landed from outer space. Jane again, invisibly.

Some girls thought winterball too mean-streaked, too psychic. My oldest daughter could hardly watch, preferring hockey. They shared a season so it was one or the other in our town. My younger daughter would rather ice-swim, but even in her ice-hole in the lake, her eyes followed Jane.

Our hearts were in Jane's feet, her hands. All the bills we couldn't pay, the wishing for electricity and lit-up screens of pleasure, the food gone rotten because no one could bring themselves to eat it—Jane gave us so many more chances to do it right this time.

We couldn't give our kids the bountiful, bullet-proof homes we wanted, but we could insist on watching them try to win their childhoods back, inspecting their scraped knees before the raw red and pink dappled wounds turned burgundy, into crusts of edible leather.

Irreversible Change

The metal fires could burn for days, glowing green without fuel, fearless. So much power was wasted on finding power sources, those electric-detectors we'd all believed in back then. They were orphans now, like us. No parent companies, no mama's lullabies.

The metal fires were art. Steel sculptures massive as ships but not ship-shaped. Spirals and spires, coils and arches, vines and limbs all gleaming with extra-terrestrial symbols. Forms only an artist with likely expensive access to divinity could understand.

An artist takes utilitarian materials and diverts that use to mystery. So that was the source of its power—it could mystically hold flame longer than any other material. A post-apocalyptic menorah, but no one was going anywhere.

A magical transmutation magically transmuted back to utility. A twice-told tale. What a strange glow it gave! Like a gargantuan spiritual generator producing for humans the light they liked best: electric-looking. Goddish. Exponential sun and stadium.

So much art was destroyed looking for more power. Paintings hooked up to electrodes, landscapes with visible landmines. Some of the better pottery bombed for phosphorescence, the blaze in their glaze. Dancers were electrocuted by semi-accident,

their choreographers' brains taken out for experiments that yielded only dead choreographers. They were the only ones who didn't watch their young stars leaping, contorted, flying up impossibly. The extensions brilliant, the velocity. Coming down meat.

Anyone who practiced their art did so secretly, and we all learned not to talk about our dreams, those visions, which could be misunderstood and burned alive. We gathered on hillsides and watched the green glow, each of us exploding with poetry silent inside.

Dream of Brown

I am dressed in brown, at a long brown wooden table set for twelve, one of many tables stretching forever. Many seats are empty, but it is mealtime. Each tabletop place is demarcated into sections, a hole for each person to sink a cup so we can barely pull it out by the slightly flared edge when we want to drink. It helps to lever it up with the thin edge of a brown wooden knife.

The shallow but persistent ridges bordering each person's eating space exist so that we don't, with our big, hungry body, spill over into someone else's space. The air is brown, and the food different shades of it, and the plates are wooden. Everything is ragged, old-looking, except for the Invisible Watchers, who enforce the rules and, I get the sense, are brand-new.

I sense this because I have been here a long time.

I am sitting in my designated space, two long spaces empty on my right and left sides. I can see you before I know it's you, but once I know it's you I can hardly look. You're so strange, dressed in a richer, stronger brown than everything else.

You sit near me, leaving still one space empty between us. I can't believe how good I suddenly feel. Excitement, possibility, hope. I think of the ways I could manage to eat in front of you, giddily, clumsily, hardly at all. And I must move closer. You might want me to—it could be—I believe you do.

queer desire?

I move my body like a pawn, one space. It's not a big move but an illegal one. Closing the space between us, I could swear there's the smallest bead of delight dropping from your face onto your lap. *deviating from the norm*

giddy energy

not supposed to be doing it

It's not long before one of the Invisible Watchers sees. A deep, Vader-like voice informs me over the loudspeaker: the seat I have stolen is already spoken for, and if I don't reclaim my original, designated space, immediately, they will give it to someone else. Then I will have no place.

gender societal roles

No place in the realm to keep myself alive, however barely. For that one spot assigned to me is the only place I am allowed to receive meals. Giving it up is suicide. I don't move. I don't move and don't move for long, long minutes. That's how I wake up every morning but this isn't a dream.

resistance

I Want the World

You never know, when you say goodbye, if it's the last time. Last time for who? For what?

Every time is the last—for that particular goodbye, wearing those clothes, at that airport. Me in my black dress—nightgown, fifties housecoat, funeral uniform. It passes for anything.

My daughter in her fuchsia track shorts and faded green t-shirt almost as soft as her luscious little arms. She was complaining, as usual. She was hungry. She was tired of traveling.

Her complaints were especially unpleasant since they only pointed up how innocent she was of how bad everything could get. The Legos are boring? Imagine no toys of any kind.

The chicken nuggets are too hot? Just wait. They'll cool and by then, I hope she can learn to like lizard blood and shoelace chewing gum, because that's what's coming.

A fierce zip of pride bites my heart. She demands more because she knows there's more in the world and she believes she should have it all. She knows what she wants: what she wants.

She believes the world is coming to her, not veering definitively away. She still thinks we can choose between ice cream flavors, bless her that she has so many possible flavors in mind.

Between stuffed animals and dolls. Which color lunch box you want for the whole school year. What school year? I think. Will first grade exist this coming fall?

She still thinks that what she thinks will affect what she gets. She still believes tantrums might get her her way. She doesn't know yet that nobody gets her way.

We're all lucky if we get anything at all, come dinnertime, come night, the next morning and the next hot morning, the next endangered livingspace if we get to stay there. We can't carry all that stuff. But she doesn't think of it as stuff.

She thinks of it as what she wants. Life's been consistent—me resisting her demands, me in my black dress, cutting my hair to make her paintbrushes. If something happens to me, who will help her believe her beliefs?

She believes her desires—as erratic and irrational as a six-year-old's desires can be —nevertheless have intrinsic value. A thread of hope wound, inextricable, all around and through her very person. I believe that, too.

One of these mornings I'll say goodbye, a routine goodbye when I go to the FedPlex warehouse to work or pick my rations, and in my absence she will lose that thread, come to fully understand what she wants is impossible in our world.

All of it, any of it, the tiniest thing, impossible.

I won't have known but I'll be walking away from my daughter for the last time, coming home (wherever home is) to someone new, someone broken off from my old girl, six years old.

Here, I tell her, providing a pencil with a pristine, unsharpened end, chew on this. Nobody's touched it yet. It's all yours, darling.

Somewhere I'll find a blade to sharpen it, and we'll find a scrap for drawing, a bit of napkin or a smooth, light stone. For now, you can chew on it. Soon you'll be able to draw whatever you want.

parents' fears
real + future

Evening Prayer for the Humans

That's not windblown hair in your eyes, it's the roots curling through you, and you've died, but it's not forever. Nothing is.

Headstones little heads peeking out the blanket.

Wood swirl looks like a yoni, auto-sexual.

Bugs don't have to be what they're not, in their spirals and blind shapes overturning, eating you.

One fever broke and now you're cooling, resting. Becoming, like the rocks, the same self as ever, this time all the way through. It was never just you.

WHAT Being dead is a lot like being alive. You don't know enough to say it, or have no way to know. Or you don't know you know—that's what being alive is like.

You don't remember—sleep was a broken egg after heavy evening sex. Ferns parted like curtains, like legs, to let you through.

sex

The streaks dried in the shape of a dragonfly.

The day was made for you to join the others. They are working already, points oscillating to drill collective holes in the Big Shroud everyone's making for everyone else equally. *Ozone?*

Others like you, unlike you. They are thirsty, and smart, and aching, waiting for you to carry their load.

Sex?

The Dessert I Didn't Have

Associations

Grilled peaches on shortbread with raspberries and black pepper ice cream.

We're all out, said the communicative waiter.

That was twelve years ago.

Why

Longing → Hope

"TO SERVE MAN": RITUALS OF
THE LATE ANTHROPOCENE COLONY

girlhood

Bakamonotako

I was thinking of changing my name to Bakamonotako. It meant The Stupid Little Octopus Girl, she was a character from an old Japanese folk tale. I read her story on a plaque outside the Little Sea Monster Museum Sculpture Garden. I thought she was a lot like me.

From a good family of upstanding octopi, Bakamonotako felt she did not need her eight appendages, she only needed four. Two to wash and work and two to walk and wander. *human*

To the embarrassment and horror of her family, she let her other four limbs fall into such disuse that they withered and fell away. So she resembled a human being, with two arms, two legs, except that her mouth and genitalia were the same orifice.

Like all stupid little girls who believe they can best become themselves by being unlike themselves, she eventually came to miss her lost limbs. At times, fully tattooed people feel so about their lost original skin.

When Bakamonotako matured and tried to have sexual relations as an adult octopus, the limbs she cast off with her mind wrapped around her and bound her, keeping her from any feeling.

Embittered and maddened by this, she consulted a wise starfish about her future. The starfish said "You must find the other half of yourself, of your private and deepest feeling, and you might have to double yourself to do it."

The starfish asked Bakamonotako for twice her usual fee for this advice, and the stupid little octopus girl paid half in sand dollars and half in sand dollars she hoped to collect in the future.

With only half her limbs, she would need to spend twice as much time scrambling in the sand on the ocean floor to find these dollars. She could see already how her fate of constantly halving and doubling was playing itself out, never to be whole, clear, even.

health care
capitalism   debt
sex

trapped

She had spent her future already, searching for sand dollars to pay the starfish for advice about her future, which had already been determined by her past.

"At this rate," thought Bakamonotako, "I'll spend my whole life looking backwards, neither living nor not living. Unless I can figure out how to accomplish the seemingly impossible task set forth by the wise starfish."

G-Bread

One of my indulgences was going to the Gingerbread House some evenings, sitting gingerly in a little gingerbread chair to eat the best g-bread. For saturation and when I could splurge the money. I felt him, one day, peeking in the sugar-frosted windows but of course he did not come in.

Perhaps he was intimidated by how intimate the place is. Too small to sit comfortably really. Or maybe by how good I smelled in it, the spice sweat-sauna ripened me as a brown paper bag will sweeten out the mealiest pear.

On religious days, of which there are many but few for me, I went to the Temple of the Three Mouths. I fed all three what they were hungry for, which took some guesswork and often-sketchy improvisations. Whatever the three mouths requested became a kind of omen for me.

Mouth One, the mouth of physicality, was the easiest. Once, it wanted peanut sauce, which made sense because it likes protein and viscosity, form and content. Mouth two twice puzzled me, once wanting a blue video and once wanting to lick my arm!

This being the mouth of love I wondered why it wanted such silly forms of it and could only guess that I came to it with deformed notions and therefore could only offer it debased versions of what I most wanted. Still, it made me sad.

The third mouth I gave whatever I could barely keep from gobbling up myself. Chocolate tomatoes and books I couldn't sleep for. Oils and petals and commotions I dreamt of on my luckiest nights. And the mouth would have none of it. I was refused every time. The mouth of abandonment.

I thought this mouth meant something and then that something was inverse. I was always baffled. Until I could penetrate the mystery, make the third mouth desire what I have to give, I would continue my supplications at the Temple.

My religious days were generally those days when my own company turned against me, when I couldn't stand myself a minute longer. What my visits to the Temple did to assuage this in-skin repulsion I don't know—and it only half-works. It was a form of religion after all.

But, after I returned home, I felt a little relief, a snake in the middle of its shedding, knowing there was still this cylinder of self left.

The Idea of Others

An animal is scritching in the wall behind my bed. At first I thought it was some kind of water crackling in a heating pipe but what kind of water stops when you thump the wall? I don't mean to be mean, I mean to make it scurry off, to send it to scritch somewhere I can't hear.

No, I'm not afraid—it is small, by the sound of its scritch. I'm not in Room 101, not worried about a gnarled whiskered rodent face chewing my eyelids in my sleep. I know these small animals, if it is an animal,

are generally afraid of big, intelligent me so far up the food chain, capable of terrible violence if frightened. I know they know they can never physically get me and are only after a crumb or a drop, like everyone really.

No, I'm trying to protect my peace of mind, my inner life, my pest-free dreams, from these unseen labors in a frenzy in the wall behind my bed. I was going to say it drives me mad and that is its fault, or was I going to say who am I to judge the urges and intensities of another species?

What I'll say instead is that I am part of the universe, privy to sounds parallel but unreachable, and on some other level, that I know I am alive, factually, unloving and alone.

WOW

Sel de la Terre, Sel de Mer

Oh funny, runny little god who lived in the sea we cut to ribbons! Tell us the big story with your infected mouth. Tell us the big story is so far beyond us we can't possibly ruin it, but you'll let us listen if we sit way in the back, quiet side creatures and marginal beasts.

We don't know what we're doing. We catch a single wave, bless you with necklaces of spit, strut ashore to pose with our medallions and titles, having won. We make little boats and toss ourselves inside like a ride on a mechanical bull. When thrown we blame the weather. *rep.*

We can't see anything in front of our face. Salt water stings and burns our eyes even when we're already crying. We cover them with plastic goggles to ogle each other underwater. We know we are aliens in too deep, but we'll never admit we don't belong.

We are the kind of storytellers that frustrate children at bedtime everywhere. "Once there was a little girl named [insert name] who was very tired and went to sleep. The end." Come on! "Okay, one more story. Once upon a time there was a blanket who was so lonely. *LOL true*

Its great wish was to one day cover up a little girl named [insert name.] Finally, after what seemed like forever and was actually way past 8:30 p.m., the girl came to bed, pulled up her blanket all cozy, and went to sleep. The end." But you can't pull one over on kids, who know when they're shorted.

Our only ways are the scammy, power-tripping ways and we know we don't deserve it but we want to hear the big story. We need an old-fashioned plume of ink, all new alphabet, to blot out our lies, all the times we were too tired, unkind, and stupid to tell the truth. *vain vs swimming*

All day a rainy day so we stay inside. That's how we see things: we close our eyes twice. That's how afraid we are of what is. When the rain stops, we dive into pools of plastic water, mistake the sexual fingers of light for fullness of heart, for the goodness of our own gooey center.

We thought we were so smart, always ahead of ourselves, minds flapping like a single flag, a mere reaction, a neural blip we thought was holy everywhere. Make us sit and listen to you. If you're at the center the center might hold.

Your countless eyes watching us, your arms radiating out in all directions, feeling for what's next. Sound comes to us in waves and we dissolve into salt water when we're most real.

Home School

SIMONE: What's "emergency cash"?

ME: Cash is money. So emergency cash is money you have in case you need it, for emergencies.

SIMONE: In case you have too much cash in an emergency, you might need money.

ME: Umm . . . no. Let me see how I can explain it. . . . If you have an emergency, you might need money, but if you don't have money you'd use emergency cash.

SIMONE: Oh! If you run out of money, you can just get more money from the emergency cash that you have?

Notes on an Old Holiday

 Old women must wear bright colors, or they disappear. Young women wear dark colors, trying to disappear and failing. Middle women are transparent, sheer to the ground.

Rivers are ancient. They think we are mosquitos they don't even bother to slap, we'll be dead so soon.

Young looks at old and thinks Old. Old looks at young and thinks Young. Neither recognizes herself as *thinking* anything. *prejudices*

We must not accept that anything is precisely what it is. Except disco pants. Those are definitely themselves. If not for you, then for your children's children.

Bitten all over my ankles by French spiders. They're leg men.

It's been twenty years since I first came to Paris. This is my eighth visit.

Twenty years ago, I was a target of men. I walked quickly, with purpose, to avoid being hit, shot, or practice. Now—and maybe since my seventh visit—I can walk slowly, thinking, at last looking at lights.

On the river, in the sky, in my own hair, silver glimmers *older* I can sense like antennae.

As a monoglot, in France, I fall back on rudimentary Japanese, a language I don't really know. Often what I need to say amounts to "okay" so I say *daijobu* while weirdly bowing in a Japanese way to a French waiter. Then, correcting, I say *c'est bon* and that must sound so stupid, to say "It's good" when a drink is spilled on me.

I don't want to be an old woman. But why not? I was sexy. I don't want to die.

It's not bad disappearing into the world if this is what the world is like.

I mean I mean that double meaning. WHAT

I never used to believe I was part of the world that meant the world to me when I was young. But it's me who changed, wasn't it? Changed what it meant?

I think my room is a little depressing. Aren't all rooms? <u>When you could be outside</u> if not for the bugs, the people, the traffic, the smell, the heat, the hot rain, the terrible sense that anything could happen to you?

11 p.m. The trees lit blue and green made me think there was still a patch of daylight. Suddenly, to have the whole day back!

If a reasonably long life, say 84 years, was divided into one single day, each hour of that day equals 3.5 years. When you are 14 years old, it's 4 a.m. When it's 10 p.m., you are 77 years old.

I'm already well past noon; I should be finishing up <u>lunch if I'm using my time well.</u>

time is $

Midnight–6 a.m.: 0–21 years. Still Dreaming

6 a.m.–noon: 21–42 years. Morning Glory

noon–6 p.m.: 42–63 years. Afternoon Delight

6 p.m.–9 p.m.: 63–73.5 years. Evening Rush

9 p.m.–midnight: 73.5–84 years. Last Call, *or find another party.*

Map of Itself

The idea of travel. The very idea.

FOUND OBJECTS/LOST SUBJECTS:

A RETROSPECTIVE

Thinking Lessons

No one is one.
No one is no one.

Is writing an act of listening?
  Or is *to listen* merely to passively search another for a portal to oneself?
    But *portal* lets anything through—and nothing stays.

I love what's sublime—beauty greater than my sense of beauty.

colors

Red is the color of surfacing, from the inside, eyes closed.

My child does not belong to me. She belongs to herself. But she's too young to have a child!

What is a new way to learn? Could I ever answer and still keep my question?

What are the most important questions, other than this one?

Our Beloved Infinite Crapulence

In Indiana, in the era of hell-wealth, way past deadline, someone on the account is sweating it, making metaphor from what is already a stretch.

And because he wants to go home to his farm-fresh slowpoke foam, grown cold, we are eventually diagnosed with winter and treated to this marketing copy off a tube of cream: "Undry Your Skin" or "A Rainforest for Your Face."

I bought it. It seemed fresh and felt organic and like it would at least wetten me, skinwise. I can't feel my old ambition to be wracked with anguish or to grow soft with loss.

When I lose, I'm still so grateful! Does that make me a chump or a champ, eating victory mussels in the lamplight of my domestic tranquility?

Gratitude often leaves me with nothing to say, as when I saw you in the toy store, I felt like a feral cat who knows only the dumpsters and the flu-scented sandboxes of now. Now that I'm happy I suppose I have to break my own heart just to feel something.

Another person with my same name goes around impersonating others; now everyone thinks I'm the impostor.

I want to tell her, "you know, you think you know me, sipping mahogany cider in the millionaire's billiards room, but there's such a thing as too much umami, and there's no way to rest forever and then go on."

Someone once said: now that I'm happy I suppose I have to break my own heart to feel something. I should remember that. I should stop praying to my dead self.

I should pull out my earbuds, and hear the world (my first love, my favorite store) without continually moving my oiled jaw hinge.

I like a chemical mysticism performed with perfect innocence. The wet slit lit up and cut down the middle, a little spit, lip a little bit split. Love in the Candle Shop: Wicked. Peeing into a Plastic Water Bottle: Wasteful. These are scents.

As is: Luck Be a Lady, So Spend Your Whole Social Security Check on Lottery Tickets Be a Gentleman. I want to smell like ceramic wind in the canyon, a brittle lust, a red-headed remedy synonymous with flooding.

Weathervane Rusted Stuck. A Stranger's Phalanges. The South Mouth. Fiercely Phlegm. Fun Old Lady. So Parachute! *WHAT*

Phrases

And now we eat. The *eponymous* eating. Don't want butter, don't want salt. Dinner is thinner but it's not my fault. We're having fungal celebrity of beef cheeks tomorrow so get yourself hungry!

For lighter fare I prefer the Soapish Fish braised in its own frothing broth, served with an aromatic retraction of statements previously made in the shade of a giant, genetically-muddled-with fiddlehead fern, infused with expelled chipmunk breath.

I . . . I love this local company, especially because for every order—and this is so cool—they make a tax-deductible contribution to honor and support the world-famous Pacific Garbage Patch, in your name.

LoL

Letters from the Elders

Dear Humans,

One word: plastics.

I won't withhold everything I've learned. I'll tell you plain. You will miss plastics.

I wish that, when people called it Cling Film instead of Saran Wrap, I'd have just let it go. It was a regional thing, not worth losing my long friendship with Mary over it.

Everything was plastic. We thought it was hygienic. We put it in our eyes so we could see better. We put plastic earbuds in our ears so we could listen ourselves out of any situation. We'd take food that was half-plastic in plastic containers, put it into another plastic container, heat it in an electric box of metal and plastic, and serve it to ourselves, guests, and families.

We'd coat each strand of our hair in plastic spray. We covered our houses, our cars, ourselves, in plastic. Every medicine, every little pill and dose had its own little plastic compartment. We stocked the reservoirs with plastic leeches which leached plastic into the water supply, so we shipped new water out to everyone in tiny plastic bottles.

The ocean was like a toddler's bathtub, plastic toys and junk everywhere, crowding out the kid, poisoning every sea. It got so even sea salt was part plastic.

But you know all about that.

We thought we were throwing it "away" until "away" threw itself back at us. This was our near-destruction, and it was well-deserved. We served it first. Some people like to point fingers but I'd like to point out that our fingers are basically plastic.

You'd press your plastic keyboard buttons all day so hard and fast the letters wore off, absorbed by your fingertips. Invisible tattoos like CRAZE and PLUM replaced your fingerprints. Babies came out with flexible plastic fingernails that fell off and grew back "natural."

If you want to know what we all could have done differently to prevent the situation we're in now, I have one word for you: everything.

Peace,
Ned "the relatively well-liked former mayor of the town formerly known as
    Peterborough, NH" Grimley-Groves

Dear Bella,

I'm writing this in case there's any chance you'll see it. If you're still alive to see this mess. I'm not sure I wish that for you as I still love you. I never stopped. Many years ago I wrote a poem for you and imagined, even though our lives took us far apart, that I would eventually have a chance to give it to you. I'd hoped one day I could read it to you in person. As it is, this is my only option. If you are reading this, I hope your life was filled with love, even if we couldn't be together. If it's not you reading this, well, I hope you enjoy the poem, whoever you are.

Mare Nostrum

The most embarrassing thing
was when you threw me
back into the water,
an old shoe you'd hooked.

It must have been, for you,
like dreaming of Italy
and waking up panicked, miserable,
on the stalled connecting red-eye. *wow*

For me it was bunions
growing in reverse, holy water
running in the gutters
I'd drink like a fish.

If I'd been more serious, kinder,
less reckless, more trustworthy,
more like you, maybe I wouldn't
have seemed like such a joke.

Ouch, is this painful, after all this time. *wow*
You must have been right
not to love me. You're practically
Italian by now and I'm still blushing.

Love forever,
Your Francesca (not my real name, but Bella—also not her real name—knows
    it's me)

Dear Humans,

It's me, again. Ned Grimley-Groves. I just had a couple more things to say, since there aren't so many places anymore that accept letters that could maybe be read by others. And I guess there aren't that many elders left anyway, which is sad. So I'll get to it.

You will miss waste. Not bio-waste, which will be everywhere since there's nowhere for it to go anymore. But you'll miss the luxurious wastefulness and the way our waste became invisible to us. Wasting everything was what kept us warm, sleeping cozily, and so clean all the time.

We were ridiculously clean, so clean it often made us sick! We'd clean our countertops with bleach and then wipe it up with a plastic sponge and soap and hot water and then throw the sponge away because bleach was toxic on surfaces our children might touch.

We'd tell our children to wash their hands after *we* cleaned the countertops. Hell, we'd tell our children to wash their hands if we saw a bug! Look, I don't know how much good it does to describe all this; we already know it. Is this for posterity? Or so the kids will know how it was?

I'm just kind of losing my momentum here. Is anyone reading this?

Well, in any case, if this "Letters from the Elders" project is ongoing, or if it reaches a wider audience, or if anyone needs me to be the editor, or to work on outreach or really anything, I am available and would love to do it.

Right now it seems to be only Francesca and me contributing letters, but if it becomes a bigger thing, or an archive of sorts, or a forum where people could communicate with each other—and you all, whoever you are, need someone—let me know! I have experience!

Sincerely,
Ned Grimley-Groves

LOL
Why

New Time Change

Individual Octopodes don't live long (between six months and two years) but as a species we have <u>extensive, meshed, intergenerational memories</u>. Humans live longer but <u>each generation forgets what was previously learned</u>.

[insert some simple way—ordinary data, culture-talk—of saying the multiple meanings here]

[use music? in algorithm? to soothe the news?]

You had your time you took your time after time you had your cake by the ocean and ate it too but now the tide has turned the times tables too when it's time to change you've got to rearrange #timesup and for old times' sake we will remember you in our time. That time is now. How soon is now. The moon is how we know.

word-play

Letter from an Elder

Dear Humans,

Hi, hi. It's Ned, again. Seems to be just me, these days. Haven't heard from Francesca, or anyone else. What did we use to say, "dance like no one is watching"? So here's a little soft-shoe—the truth can't hurt us now. How sad that we once thought it could; told early enough it might have saved us.

Or maybe we have been saved, too soon to tell. Obviously I miss the technology and the speed, traveling and inventions, the way teenagers were finding simple cures for quickly mutating viral diseases. I miss that direction, sure. I miss movies and weddings, office-pals, my grandma, my kids, buying what I wanted. I even miss saving up to buy what I wanted. I miss anticipation, goals. Interminable dance recitals that no one watched because they were recording them on devices.

We were quite literally gunning for our own extinction, it now seems obvious. If not by pandemic, or self-inflicted extreme climate events, or border/nation hysteria, gleefully murderous cops and presidents and dictators, the infinite variations of pollution and cruelty and deliberate ignorance—we threw children in prison, we let them be sold—and who was "we"? we wonder, now that we are no longer us. *key*

But nothing dehumanized us like the guns. The endless guns in anybody's hands were always someone else's fault. Every trigger finger pointed at someone else, in a war against someone else. We hated anyone we thought wasn't like us, but of course we were all like us. We hated ourselves. We chose evil, elected it, protected it, let it maim the animals, steal the land, drop the bombs, poison the water, terrorize the children, fund the greedy, and squander every last chance.

We let guns kill our children on a daily basis. Who are we to say the Octopodes did anything worse? They're an ink species. They overwrote us. They dissembled our guns by dissolving our systems in the middle of our own shoot-out. What we thought was gun smoke was ink cloud. The writing was never on the wall, it was in the water. Our names, like Keats's, writ there.

Of course they'll never understand us. Have *we* ever understood us? We were the humans, a bafflement of evolution: most species evolve to live; we devolved to evil. Most infinitesimal specks get squashed by a much bigger foot, and maybe we're not the only dot of a species to die of its own self-hatred, but we are rare. We were rare. The lovely planet may be salvaged with our extinction—I won't live to know, but it would be some last light. ☆

I cling to this because to hope for this earth to go on after we're gone is the only kind of love left—the last good human piece of us. That some of our ether, soul, spirit, wishes, vibrations might linger here. That some form of hope can stay, with or without us.

And if not, maybe the Octopodes will care to find some form to remember us by. In case that is the case, I am collecting fragments—scraps I find here and there in script or print, among the debris, mostly anonymous ephemera and some poetry, which surprises me. I didn't think we wrote poetry much anymore.

I remain available, for now, at my new address.

Ned Grimley-Groves
(formerly of New Hampshire)
Salinization Pod #11298 N.E.

Nest

Cal's not doing so well, and I can't think straight.
It's almost his birthday, and I'm not home to be
with him. I'm in a cabin up in the New Hampshire
woods, in order to write. I'm writing this.

Craig was up with him most of last night, he said.
Cal was coughing and gagging, probably allergies,
and this happens every spring. But today Cal's nurse
says he was wheezing and had a rough day at school,
his temperature a little up and now the babysitter

is taking Cal, Simone tagging along, to the doctor,
and Craig is leaving work early to meet them there,
to make sure Cal is okay. Albuterol, Benadryl, Motrin
don't seem to be helping. Maybe he needs a stronger

allergy medicine, something prescription? Craig
will tell me as soon as the doctor tells him.
Right before Craig told me all this, I was reading
the end of a novel about a rich man who lost
everything and was going to his home country

to see if he could reclaim anything there, his birthright
and family property seized and stolen in the forties.
He arrived in Beijing and is wandering around, light-
headed from not eating and from fear. I didn't

finish the book because I heard a buzzing. A wasp
I was sure was on the outside of the screened-in
porch was in. I thought we could co-exist peacefully
for a few minutes but then I thought about coming
back at night, or forgetting about it in the morning

and I didn't want to be afraid. I decided that since
I knew where it was, could see it on the screen,
and that I had a good shot right now, I should get it.
It's a wasp, I thought. It's not a good bug like a bee

or a spider. It's a bad bug, and will sting me if it can.
I thought I got a good weapon, a stiff cardboard box.
I didn't want to use anything heavier, what if I broke
the screen? I steadied myself and pushed the flat
flat against the wasp, which pushed back more than

I thought it would, and it dropped and I dropped
the box. I couldn't see it. Did I get it? I fled inside
and closed the door. Maybe it's injured, maybe
just hiding. Heart pounding, I'm peering through

the window trying to see. I can't see anything, just
the box I dropped. I don't know how I'm going
to get out of here now. I think if that wasp is still
alive it will surely be out to get me. It's strange that
just a moment ago I was so calm, so immersed.

Not a minute after I found myself trapped, my phone
buzzed. It doesn't get much reception but the text
from Craig came through and that's when I learned
that Cal wasn't doing so well, and all the info I said

above, which is all the info I have at this point.
I know Cal will be okay. But how do I know it?
Do I know it simply because it has to be true?
Or because Craig says he's not that worried?
Or does Craig say he's not that worried because

he doesn't want to worry me? Why am I up here
writing in the woods when my family needs me
if all I'm doing is failing to kill innocent wasps
and writing this, this poem I'll never really finish.

This poem I stole from my fear, my endless fear.
I don't want to find the wasp dead. I want it to live,
to find its way outside this poem, away from me
and the fear I know will find me again. I'll go
home to my son, three days before he turns ten.

Blueberries for Cal

Watching little Henry, six, scoop up blueberries
and shovel them into his mouth, possessed.

I'm so glad I brought blueberries—wish my kids
could/would eat them. Cal can't; Simone won't.

Henry's sisters Lucy & Jane took turns feeding each
other goldfish crackers and sips of juice.

Arms around each other's neck and back. Tiny things.
I wish my daughter had a sister like that

and my son a nervous system that let him walk
and munch berries. Sometimes I can't bear

all the things Cal doesn't get to do. I want to curse
everything I can't give him.

Admire/compare/despair—that's not the most real
feeling I'm feeling, is it? I feel joy in Henry's joy.

Blueberries for the child who wants them.
There's all this energetic sweetness, enough to go around,

to give and taste and trust. More than enough.
For Cal, too. I want to remember this.

My children seem to subsist on music and frosting.
Where there's frosting, there's cake.

Where there's music, someone chose to make a song
over all other things on this earth.

PERMANENT COLLECTION: ARCHIVE
OF PRE-EXISTING CONDITIONS

Are Women People?

A report commissioned by the COP's Department of Human Studies. In the interest of anthropological authenticity, cephalopod researchers utilized only methods and modes used by humans themselves, in their various legal, academic, and socio-cultural institutions. To the best of our ability, we worked within their language and wielded their tools in order to better understand their mysteries, and how to serve mankind's legacy. —the authors   *Ha!*

1. FRAMING THOUGHTS:

We don't believe the question in the report's title to be self-evident.

Governing documents use this term, *self-evident,* so it seems legit, foundational, but it's a pleonasmic tautology, a proud cheese full of holes, a question answered untruly by itself, palindrome-like: Is it real? Real it is!

To begin to understand how to answer the question we must define the two terms: *women* and *people. People* is a broader term than *women.* Women are a subset of people. Women are a kind of people.

People are not a kind of women.

At this moment someone will always say: men are also a subset of people! It goes the other way, too! People who need to interject that point are usually men. When you hypothetically posit the word *women* as a term that includes men (logical, as the word *men* is already there within the word *women*) in practice the terms lose all meaning.

Men found it insulting and risky not to be named as the sole primary term—it seemed wrong, their personhood status implied but not fully legally inscribed. And it was deemed too clunky to have to say *men and women* every single time a reference was made to people, so *women* became the secondary term, an addendum to the word *men.*

To recap: *People* includes both men and women. *Man* claims to include women, but doesn't. *Woman* doesn't include men, or women as a group. *Man* is plural, encompassing humanity (which, clearly, serves man). *Woman* is singular, individual. To each her own.   *INT*

2. QUERIES: HOW DO WE DEFINE PEOPLE?

Does a person have to be a human being?
Are animals people?
Are corporations people?
Are ideas people?
Are objects made by humans people?
Are fictional characters people?

What about past people?
Are dead people still people?
Are people who exist in memory only, names inscribed on stones or buildings, people?
Are people who only exist in wills and legal terms people?
Are the wishes and requests of dead people people?
Are ghosts, once they've been proven to exist, people?

What about future people?
Are children people?
Are babies people?
Are unborn babies people?
Are fetuses people?
Are embryos people?
Are zygotes people?
Are sperm people?
Are ova people?
Are people's plans to have children people?
Are the ova of people's children people?
Are the ova of people's unborn babies people?
Are the ova of fetuses people?
Are the ova of embryos people?
Are the undifferentiated cells that may become ova or sperm people?
Are the undifferentiated cells that may become people who may become parents to
    people who may become parents to people who may become parents to people
    who may become parents people?

If there's a possibility that essential parts (undifferentiated cells, for example) of
    people are in themselves also people, then are other essential parts also people?
Is a human brain people?
Is a human heart people?

Is human waste people?

Is human emotion people?

Is human ingenuity people?

Is human survival instinct people?

Is the basic luck to be born at all people?

Is DNA people?

Is a torso people?

Is a neck people?

If it's possible that essential parts are people, might non-essential parts be people?

Is a foot people?

Are seeing or unseeing eyes people?

Is human sexual arousal people?

Is a human sense of humor people?

Is language people?

Is talent people?

Are mental disorders people?

Are diseases people?

Is a photograph that captures the essence of a person and allows that person to live on in human memory people? (i.e., a child pointing to a photo, saying, "That's Grandma!")

What about people for whom essential or non-essential parts are absent? Are they people? Are parts of them people, but not other parts? Is it possible to be part people/part non-people?

Are humans with artificial body parts people?

Are humans who hurt other humans without remorse people?

Are humans who cannot take care of themselves people?

Are humans who are chemically dependent people?

Are humans who are terminally ill people?

Are humans who lack melanin people?

Are humans who lack compassion people?

Are humans who have impaired function (physical, mental, emotional) people?

Are humans who do not use language people?

Are humans who could survive in the wild with no human interaction people?

Are loners people?

Are people who can't learn people?

Are people who don't want to learn people?

———

Are people who hold positions of power in governance, law enforcement,
   or other hierarchies that control the lives and freedom of people people?
Are members of Congress people? (Is the State people?)
Are police people? (Is the embodiment of law enforcement, to which people must
   submit, people?)
Are scientists people? (Is someone first and foremost beholden to the data people?)
Are engineers/programmers who only work with machines, never humans,
   people? (Are machines people?)
Are dancers people? (Are humans who primarily use their bodies for art people?)
Are artists people? (Is someone for whom aesthetic questions are primary people?)

3. SPECIAL STATUS: CHILDREN

Children are, at the very least, future people, but anything could happen.

They could be female, and a good half of them do end up as such, so children are
just as likely to become future women (not people) as they are to become people.

They could belong to a religion, and depending on which one, this might make
them god's people, not people-in-themselves. For example: the Christian god in
particular does not share, so Christians are not people, they are god's.

In the case of Buddhists, their god shares them and they share their god, but
as they share themselves with everyone and all, belonging to none—not even
themselves—they cannot be claimed as, or to be, people.

There are many such cases to be considered.

4. SPECIAL STATUS: PEOPLE OF COLOR

Depending on geography or parental heritage, having brown or dark skin, skin
which does not usually change even over a long life, these factors . . .

these factors, in and of themselves, have no bearing on whether or not they are
people . . .

but certain circumstances present obstacles

to their inclusion

Mere origin or heritage or skin color is not in and of itself considered a factor

and in the case of mixed-heritage, or dual-country-of-origin, there are complexities

to consider the fixities of legal terms, to honor existing definitions where they do exist

Let it be stated that People of Color, taking into account all the variables and contingencies, are certainly people (unless they are women or future people—a separate category with variables and contingencies as argued above and below).

These people are a category in and of themselves— a kind of people obligated to continually renew their licenses, registrations, residencies, identification papers, passports, bank account information, school enrollment, property deeds or rental leases, birth and death certificates, health benefits, medical forms and records, utility accounts, social security data, employment records, political party affiliations.

These documents must be continually updated to protect the status of People of Color as people.

These documents are and records are proof that dark-skinned people, brown people, people who come from Countries of Color or who have one or more parents from Countries of Color are people, and it is incumbent upon them to keep all records and data updated, renewed, and accurate.

This is all for their own protection.

There is a long history of fraudulence, misinformation, identity theft, impersonation, money laundering, forged documents, improper registration, multiple claims, and other illegal activity, and so vigilance is required to protect People of Color's status as people.

Legal offenses, such as criminal activity and association with violence, can result in the individuals forfeiting their access to this system of registration and renewal required to extend their status as people in perpetuity. If individuals enter the prison or corrections systems as perpetrators of crimes, they can no longer uphold the obligation of being people, and the status of personhood can be revoked.

Outside the judicial and correctional systems, it's possible to default on that status as well. Simply forgetting to renew registrations or any of the above documents can render questionable/null/void an individual's status in the group known as people. Crimes are defined as any "illegal activity" and this includes any lapses in registrations or expired documents.

5. REPRODUCTIVE FUNCTIONS AND MANAGEMENT OF MEN AND WOMEN

Differences between men and women are primarily physical. Socialization, legislation, education, and segregation have codified, altered, and enhanced those physical differences, it seems, in the interest of people. *really?*

1. People are physically born out of the bodies of women.
2. Male sperm are required to start new human life, but sperm can be separated from men, stored indefinitely, used at will, without any need for the rest of the physical man.
3. Female ova can also be harvested, frozen, implanted separately from the woman, but no artificial replacement has been found for the gestation of the embryo. This forty-week period of gestation can only occur in the body of a living woman. There is currently no medical or scientific research advocating the creation of artificial gestational systems.
4. Women are required to make People
   a) this has been interpreted in two ways
      i) "women, inseparable from their bodies, are essential to making people."
      ii) "women are obligated/compelled to make people." *Int.*
5. Men are not required to make people
   a) this has been interpreted in two ways
      i) "men, whose reproductive contribution is easily and painlessly extractable from their bodies, are inessential to making people."
      ii) "men are not obligated/compelled to make people." *Int.*
6. People are dependent on women to continue making people. Such a small percentage of women are (1) of childbearing age, (2) able to bear children, and (3) want to bear children. Some

estimate that only 7–10% of the total population are women who
meet all three criteria to bear children.

7. For the benefit of all people to ensure their survival and
   continuation of the human species, women's reproductive
   systems—inasmuch as they are inseparable from women as
   beings—are of collective special interest to the people, and can
   be said to be "held in trust" of the people.

8. For survival and continuation of the people themselves, the
   people are the Trustees of the reproductive capacities of women
   between the ages of thirteen and fifty. Women of childbearing
   age and ability cannot be said to have full control over their
   bodies, as they may not qualify as Trustees, if they are not
   proven to be people.

9. This document seeks to discover whether women can be proven
   to be people.

10. In the event that proof cannot be obtained that women are
    people, women will be held indefinitely (or until proof can be
    obtained) in a "pre-status" category. "Pre-status" status confers
    no rights of people-hood, which are deferred until the required
    documentation is obtained, received, and validated.

6. CONCLUSION:

Based on our research, it appears the definition of "human" is unstable, and so is
that of the plural synonym "people." Human parts may or may not be "people"
and as "women" are a part of the term "people" they may or may not qualify
in and of themselves. It has been discovered that a tiny minority of humans can
legally, fully occupy the category of people (with most of the population falling
in the subcategories of Special Status and Women) and this minority is deeply
endangered, growing more minuscule as time passes. It has been established that
women are occasionally people, depending on circumstances that can change. This
is primarily because they are essential to the survival of the human species and
therefore they paradoxically are (1) the seat, crux, and essence of people as well as
(2) too essential in their reproductive capacity to be allowed full personhood—their
bodies must be held in trust by the state (which confers personhood) in pre-status
from ages thirteen to fifty in order to preserve the future of potential people. In the
cases that women are also in "Special Status" categories as people of color and/or
children, further contingencies apply.

Honeymoon

It's so flat here you can see everything. It's not romantic. Nobody can slip in or out in secret, and who among us has pumped the last worry through her heart?

Collapsing into shade, I wish for more sons, endless daughters: a higher ratio of my people to other people. Why not want what I want; since we used all the air conditioning it's become impossible to think things through.

Can you believe your ears? All the electric music in the world has been turned into handbells. I wish I had a cushion for my knees instead of gloves to keep the handbells pure. We can get used to anything. That doesn't mean we should.

I went to a wedding where everything was outrageous but trying to act modest by including very goofy elements, such as people in bear costumes and gold nuggets descending from the ceiling, only to be jerked back up out of reach when people tried to grab them.

Long ago, a matrimonial family collected a few eggs from each household in the village to contribute to the wedding cake. A pig for the dinner: a gift from a rich great-uncle. Shortly after, there was a period of department store gift services and electro-synth harps for hire.

But now we pick dandelions to make wine, and pluck chickens to make fine the groom's cloak. He wants large brown wings; he wants wolf pelt for his loins. He wants he wants he wants. There is no end to that.

The bride is someone who has only ever served. No use asking someone who's once had a true taste of freedom, whose eyes widened and whose pelvis thrust up unbidden. Better she be someone who might never know what she lost.

It is as it ever was. How many centuries have brides been made and used in this way?

How few centuries have let women be girls first, swirling as long as they wanted into their sweetness and sharpening to ripeness, only becoming women once full heavy love was their desire inside and out. Maybe one. Maybe not quite one full century.

Our Zero Waiver

Her head in my lap, looking up at the sky. I watched her face watch the stars, moon lighting her like a still lake. I couldn't tell what color her eyes were; they could be light ordinarily but collected all the dark tickets to ride the night in peace, in calm, tonight.

I brushed her hair away from her forehead. I don't think she's happy, but her worries have smoothed, it seems. How could she be happy? She came to us under an inhuman law and I have no idea what she suffered. She's somewhere between thirty-eight and forty-two, and she had nowhere to go.

We took her in. We don't have much but we couldn't bear the feeling of hoarding our one extra bedroom, since Nana died. We figured we'd volunteer for a minus-one/plus-one Zero Waiver, instead of waiting and watching the household rations be cut due to decreased household size.

No, we aren't so selfless a family. I'll never know if we would have been. If things were different, would we have taken in foster children, adopted orphaned or abandoned babies? Opened our doors, arms aching to give love where love was needed?

Instead of waiting for them to reassess our unit, for them to size us up for an assigned new occupant, we figured if we volunteered at least we could choose the category. That way we'd be assigned a woman between the ages of thirty-eight and forty-two (there's a surplus).

I was mostly worried we'd get assigned an Offender. A man. Someone who lied and broke down doors and would keep us sleepless. We couldn't choose who'd come to live with us but we could avoid an Offender if we took on an Early Crone.

We were allowed an EC because we're not allowed another non-Offender man. It's why we couldn't take in our friend Paul, who needed a home. Our old neighbor Michelle could have been safe with us but she's too young. Until age thirty she'll live in the Young Women's Space.

You get someone who doesn't know you, usually from another town. Someone who probably has to leave for any of the usual reasons—a baby is born or a family member is released back into the home. Sometimes it's her own baby. Sometimes a sibling returns.

There are unofficial "occupancy-matchmakers" more broker than seer. They know many people in a lot of single-family-occupancy housing, and folks tell them the news, the comings and goings. Welch was our broker.

We gave her daughter reading lessons for a year as soon as Nana got sick, payment in advance for finding us a good woman of the right age and circumstance. It was almost too much to hope for to find someone remotely stable or sane. Show me one person who is these days—that's a clone.

She brought Amy to our place one week ago. Amy's been crying a lot, and then stone-faced, and then apologetic, her misery genuine, her smile forced. She must have had a baby she had to leave, or the baby died. In any case, her milk came in.

My heart broke for her. Nobody's allowed to waste baby milk but fuck it—not everything can be salvaged, inventoried, sold. Together we went out to the back yard near the trees and lay down on our backs. I didn't want to touch her. How tender she must be.

But she propped her head onto the pillow of my lap, better to see the stars and moon. I sat up then, the better to watch her. My skirt was wet in two spots from her tears. Her shirt was wet in two spots from her milk. My own cheeks were streaked, my eyes mirrored, shadowed, by her shining ones.

The night was celebrating its sparkles, moonglow, glimmering, showing off like TV shows used to show themselves at night, exposing themselves in our living rooms. She and I made no sound, said nothing. What would we say? Who could hear it in that loud night flashing its millions of bodies?

Our Family on the Run

Everything organized around Cal in his wheelchair. He can't walk and I can't carry him far. We'd have the wheelchair van, as long as we could find gas. Simone in the side seat, Craig and me in the front.

Maybe spray paint a Super Soaker metallic silver to look like a real weapon?

Load the car up with cans of enteral food for Cal's G-tube. Maybe a six-week supply, plus a go-backpack full of cans, extensions, spare Mic-Key button. Three days of food for the rest of us. We'll find water.

Sleeping in the front seats, taking turns on watch. Simone curled up next to the gas can and ziplock of batteries/cords/chargers, with her one stuffed animal we have to worry about something happening to, her only toy.

And what if we lose the car? Running on some side road to— Pennsylvania/airport/Atlantic/evacuation center/relocation camp/as yet unknown. Trying to buy a blow-up raft for four people. Can't take the wheelchair.

Our stack of euros to buy four plane tickets: can't take the wheelchair.

On foot, trying to get to a friend's country home, promise of a bedroom. No way to call the friend for directions. A compass one of the kids got at a birthday party wound up under a car seat. Lucky.

Lucky, too, Simone can walk—though she gets tired and I'd want to hoist her on my back if I didn't have to save my energy to carry Cal when Craig's legs give way, his back out.

Cal, four foot six and sixty pounds of tween, who must be carried if we somehow lose that wheelchair. Or the wheelchair breaks, or is stolen, or gets a flat tire, or rusts.

It's red, a color Cal chose by smiling when we said "red" in a list of colors. No expression when we said blue, green, black, purple, or pink. Big smile when we said red. He had his choice and he made it.

How strange that the color of his wheelchair ever mattered enough to anyone to offer him that handful of options.

Simone is hungry. I give her a Clif bar (that twenty-four pack I bought for rushed mornings) and she drops half of it on the dirt road, which is covered in, what, bone dust or atomized drywall?

She grabs what she dropped and stuffs it into her mouth before I can stop her. Why would I stop her?

The side of the road is the well-known gutter of desperation always included in stories about wars where many people have to move on foot to the next terrible place.

No matter what the emergency, whenever people are forced to flee you find, piece by piece, how their understanding of their situation changed.

If you read the stories, you're supposed to find abandoned photo albums, suitcases, babies. The useless things cut out by survival's swift knife. Dead weight, long gone.

You never find food, bottled water, working flashlights, live batteries, shortwave radios. It's true, what all those stories said, it turns out.

Eventually out of water and arms shredded, I carry Cal, Craig carries me, and Simone carries us all. Almost seven years old, she is so strong and has some Clif bars stuffed in a bag. The notebook with all our information is long lost.

She knows where she's going. How does she know that? She runs ahead and carries us, her heart pounding and breaking with the weight and strain of all of us in there.

ACKNOWLEDGMENTS

Gratitude to the editors and staff of the magazines and periodicals that published the following poems: "Honeymoon" in *Poetry* magazine. "Gift Planet" in *The New Yorker*. "Bakamonotako" in *granta.com.* "The Home Team" on *Poem-a-Day* by The Academy of American Poets. "No Traveler Returns," "There Was No Before," and "Are Women People?" in *American Poetry Review*. "Identity & Community," "Sel de la Terre, Sel de Mer," and "Our Beloved Infinite Crapulence" in *Berkeley Poetry Review*. "Blueberries for Cal," "Wellness Rituals," and, in modified form, "Evening Prayer for the Humans" in *Paris Review*. "Wellness Rituals" was written for Jessica Rankin's 2017 solo exhibition at Touchstones Art Gallery in Rochdale, U.K.

These poems were inspired by reading Emily St. John Mandel's novel *Station Eleven* and Peter Godfrey-Smith's *Other Minds: The Octopus, The Sea, and the Deep Origins of Consciousness.*

This book owes its existence to The MacDowell Colony (where I wrote most of it) and Civitella Ranieri (where I finished it). Gratitude to The Vermont Studio Center, Denniston Hill, Provincetown FAWC, and the American Academy of Arts and Letters. Thank you so much for the various essential gifts of time, peace, space, and/or funds.

Appreciation and thanks beyond words to my colleagues and students at Rutgers University–Newark; beyond words, too, is the grief of losing beloved Jan Ellen Lewis, our Dean of Arts and Sciences, who championed writers, who cared so deeply about supporting us and the work of literature.

Love to those good eggs in my home community in NJ—I don't believe they know how much they helped me write this book, in particular Kate Francis Hardy, Reubena Spence, Addie Morfoot, and Ross Kauffman. To Wendy Gould-Nogueira: you inspire me every day—how I wish you ran the world.

Poets, friends, mentors, coconspirators who gave me hope post-2016 election: Robin Coste Lewis, Rachel Eliza Griffiths, Natalie Diaz, Rigoberto Gonzalez, Mark Bibbins, John Keene, Jessica Rankin, Deborah Landau, Tayari Jones, Suzanne Buffam, Robyn Schiff, Ellis Avery, Monica Youn, Eliza Factor, Amy Herzog, Elizabeth Gold, Mark Wunderlich, Dana

Cadman, Urvashi Vaid, Kate Clinton, Wendy Brown, Fran Bartkowski, Paola Prestini, EnactLab, and my adored Pretendettes.

Two mentors who shaped me, Lucie Brock-Broido and Helene Moglen, died, and I didn't say good-bye. So I'll say it here, with an infinite thank-you. I know what I learned from you made me a writer. Grateful that you lived and taught. I was so lucky to receive what you gave.

I cannot thank Deborah Garrison enough for her wise, true guidance, clear eye, and for always leading with heart and mind entwined.

Admiration, praise, and thanks to Todd Portnowitz, Nimra Chohan, Kelly Forsythe, and Leslie Shipman for making heavy lifting seem like smooth sailing.

To Craig: there's no one I'd rather share kids, home, life, strife, self, and poetry with. In case of apocalypse: that too, I know, will be better with you. I love you.

NOTES

The title "Map of Itself" belongs to Craig Teicher, who lent it to me here.
The poem "Nest" refers to the plot of the novel *Wangs vs. the World* by Jade Chang

A NOTE ABOUT THE AUTHOR

Brenda Shaughnessy was born in Okinawa, Japan, and grew up in Southern California. She is the author of four books of poetry, including *So Much Synth*, *Human Dark with Sugar*— winner of the James Laughlin Award and finalist for the National Book Critics Circle Award—and *Our Andromeda,* which was a *New York Times Book Review* "100 Notable Books of 2013." She is an associate professor of English at Rutgers University, Newark. She lives in New Jersey.

A NOTE ON THE TYPE

Pierre Simon Fournier *le jeune* (1712–1768), who designed the type used in this book, was both an originator and a collector of types. His services to the art of printing were his design of letters, his creation of ornaments and initials, and his standardization of type sizes. In 1764 and 1766 he published his *Manuel typographique,* a treatise on the history of French types and printing, on typefounding in all its details, and on the measurement of type by the point system.

Composed by North Market Street Graphics, Lancaster, Pennsylvania

Printed and bound by Thomson-Shore, Inc., Dexter, Michigan

Designed by Maggie Hinders